Cry Softly!
The Story of Child Abuse

Cry Softly!
The Story of Child Abuse

Revised and Enlarged

Margaret O. Hyde

The Westminster Press
Philadelphia

Book design by Gene Harris

Published by The Westminster Press®
Philadelphia, Pennsylvania

PRINTED IN THE UNITED STATES OF AMERICA
9 8 7 6 5 4 3 2 1

Library of Congress Cataloging-in-Publication Data

Hyde, Margaret Oldroyd, 1917–
  Cry softly!

  Bibliography: p.
  Includes index.
  Summary: Discusses child abuse, its history in England and America, ways to prevent and stop it, and how to report suspected cases.
    1. Child abuse—Juvenile literature.   2. Child abuse—United States—History—Juvenile literature.   [1. Child abuse]   I. Title.
  HV713.H98 1986   362.7′1   85-31462
  ISBN 0-664-32723-0

Contents

1

Cry Softly,
Keep the Secret,
or Leave the House

Each day, untold numbers of children, victims of child abuse, cry softly to hide their hurt from the outside world. Some victims do not cry at all, for these children, victims of sexual abuse, are told to keep the "game" a secret unless they want terrible things to happen. For others, the abuse involves neglect that ranges from minor to complete. Many abused children are told to leave the house, even when they have no place to go. They join the homeless who try to survive "life on the street," and the street is a brutal parent.

Many forms of child abuse have become popular causes for people who are concerned about the rights and welfare of children. But recent estimates suggest that between two thousand and five thousand children die each year as a result of assault by their adult caregivers, and a million, or perhaps five million, suffer from some form of abuse. As

7

many as twelve children suffer permanent brain damage each day from abuse, and it is estimated that every two minutes a child is attacked by one or both parents. A study from the National Committee for Prevention of Child Abuse points out that 97 percent of hard-core delinquents experienced a history of child abuse and 80 percent of prison inmates have been abused as children.

The true extent of family violence is just beginning to surface. As many victims learn that they are not alone, they are coming forward in growing numbers. This is especially true in the case of sexual abuse. Experts estimate that one in four female children and one in six male children will be molested or raped by the time they reach adulthood. But sexual abuse is probably the least common kind of abuse. Estimates of a million or more children suffering from physical or emotional abuse each year are considered low.

No one is certain of the magnitude of the maltreatment of children, but there is increasing evidence that child abuse is a huge and terrible problem in our society. Despite recent publicity and the introduction of child abuse prevention as a current priority, the number of victims appears to be increasing. For example, the state of Vermont recently reported an increase of 77 percent in the annual number of substantiated cases of abuse. While experts attributed part of the increase to better reporting, there are indications that actual abuse has increased both there and in many other parts of the country.

Today, doctors, teachers, and others who work with children are alert to symptoms of physical abuse and are required to report it. When four-year-old Billy was brought to the hospital with severe bruises from being beaten with the heel of his mother's shoe, the mother's story of a fall was questioned. Even though she often told Billy to cry softly so the neighbors would not hear him, the caretakers at his day-care center were alerted to the problem of physical abuse when Billy's body showed frequent bruises. The day he was taken to the hospital was the day that a social worker began to work with his mother in an effort to help her deal with her anger in less harmful ways.

Six-year-old Betsy was not as fortunate as Jimmy. She was abused in a way that was less obvious. When Betsy displeased her mother, she was tied to her bed. Sometimes Betsy's mother would go out for long periods of time and leave Betsy tied in such a way that she could not get up. When her mother returned, she would tell Betsy she was sorry she had left her so long. She would buy Betsy presents, give her sodas and candy, and tell Betsy she had meant to untie her before leaving for the party.

Time and time again, Betsy was neglected, but

she was afraid to complain to her teacher for fear she would be taken away from her mother. Betsy did not know that she and her mother could be helped without being separated. She just hoped that her mother would treat her better in the future. Unfortunately, this is never very likely unless the case is reported and counseling is made available.

Eight-year-old Todd lived with a family who thought they provided him with the best of everything. He was well fed, his health care was excellent, and he had a tremendous supply of educational toys and books. Todd did not get along well in school, even though intelligence tests showed that he was extremely bright. He fought with the other children, and he was too restless in the classroom to keep up with the work. Neither the teacher nor Todd's parents could understand his behavior. They did not realize that his father was the cause of his stress. Todd's father demanded perfect behavior. When Todd displeased his father, the boy was ridiculed. When Todd won a game, his father called him an egghead, and when he lost, his father made fun of him and called him stupid. No matter how hard Todd tried to please his father, he never could. He was the butt of his father's jokes and was put down on every occasion. Todd's father felt that this treatment would keep Todd on his toes. The father never realized that he was abusing the boy emotionally.

Grace appeared to be a runaway teenager, but the social worker who talked to her soon learned that she was a "throwaway," a child not wanted at home. Her stepfather made it clear that he would beat her if she did not put up with his sexual advances. After overhearing him tell her mother that she was in their way, Grace ran away, hoping to find a job in the city. She was frightened until she happened to see a notice pasted on the door of a phone booth suggesting a call to a runaway hotline. Before long, she was living in a center for runaways, where the social worker promised to help her find a job and a place to live.

Carol is the victim of a new kind of child abuse. Her mother wants her to claim that her father abuses her sexually when she spends weekends with him. Her mother wants to use lies to change the custody arrangement, and Carol finds this situation very difficult. She must continue to live most of her life with her mother who is abusing her without realizing it.

Five-year-old Bobby is the victim of yet another kind of child abuse, one that has not always been recognized as such. He was kidnapped by his father in order to spite his mother after she was given custody of the boy. Bobby's father has told him that his mother does not want to see him again because she has remarried and her new husband's children have moved into the house. Bobby and his father move around a great deal, and he even has to dress like a girl sometimes. All of this confuses Bobby, who does not realize that his mother is searching for him.

Bobby is just one of hundreds of thousands of children who are kidnapped by noncustodial parents each year. Child snatching is a crime in many states. In many cases, physical or emotional abuse was the cause of the divorce. In each case, the child who is abducted suffers some form of abuse.

Child abuse does not always fall into neat categories, for many children suffer from more than one form. However, kinds of abuse are often described as physical abuse (including neglect), emotional abuse, or sexual abuse.

Definitions of child abuse vary somewhat. According to the U.S. Congress, it is "the physical or mental injury, sexual abuse, negligent treatment or maltreatment of a child under the age of eighteen by a person who is responsible for the child's welfare under circumstances which indicate that the child's health or welfare is harmed or threatened thereby."

A number of definitions of child abuse show a growing understanding of the abuser. One is "a family crisis which threatens the physical or emotional survival of a child." Such views are the result of an effort to identify the causes of the problem as well as to treat the symptoms of the child. It might be possible to help the family in such a way that the abuse would not continue to happen. Since abuse is seldom just a single happening, such as a parent's simple burst of rage, the problem is far deeper than healing a broken leg or other easily seen injury.

Perhaps no mother wakes up thinking that she is going to batter her child. Who would do such a horrible thing? A father who punishes his child by burning an arm with his cigarette probably does not know that there are better ways to teach about fire. Who are these people who tell their children to cry softly so the neighbors will not hear them?

2

Who Are
the Child Abusers?

Although child abusers are often thought of as monsters, they are really people who desperately want and need help, even though they may not know it. If you stood in a crowd and looked around, you could not pick out the child abusers. However, they *are* different.

Are these people suffering from a mental illness that distorts their thinking? Are they mean people who cannot understand that hurting children is a horrid thing to do? What causes people to abuse their children? Why would anyone behave this way?

You may know child abusers without realizing it. They come from all groups in society. They belong to all races, religions, and ages and to both sexes. A child abuser may be the man who lives down the street. Call him Mr. Jones. He goes to work each day, speaks pleasantly but shyly to you when you meet him on the street, and looks like a person who could never harm a living thing. Inside the house, this man is part of a family under stress. He never felt loved as a child, and he was unable to love his own children. One of the children, Mary, is especially troublesome as far as Mr. Jones is concerned. She looks somewhat like the sister he always hated, and she was born at a time when he was under great stress at work. She always seemed to be crying when he came home from work. Why couldn't Mary behave? Why couldn't she show how much she loved him? His sister never showed any love for him, and this child was going to be just like her.

Actually, Mr. Jones expects too much of Mary. He expects her to provide the love he missed as a child, and he cannot understand that Mary is too young to provide grown-up comfort and love.

When Mr. Jones beats Mary, she cries even more. The mother tries to protect the child, but she feels her first duty is to her husband. She decides that Mary is young and will forget the severe beatings. Her body will heal fast. When people ask about the bruises on Mary's body, the mother finds excuses for them. Most of the time, she can cover the red marks with clothing. Mr. Jones continues to pass as a fine, considerate man.

What kind of person would harm a child? Certainly there must be many abusive parents, and just as certainly each person and each case is different from every other one.

In their efforts to prevent abuse, many men and women who study this problem have suggested traits that are common among child abusers. This does not mean that everyone who has these traits is a child abuser or that a child abuser must have all these traits.

Almost 10 percent of the people who hurt children are so severely troubled that there is little chance of helping them to overcome their problem. Some of this 10 percent do not live in the real world, but in a world that exists only in their imaginations. Some hear voices and are very confused in their thinking. The child may be considered as a force of the devil, as a threat, or in some other unreal way. A very severely depressed parent may not have the energy or the ability to take care of a child. This is one reason for neglect.

It has been suggested that child abuse is one way people have of asking for help. Abusive parents are usually unable to reach out for help the way most people can, for they have lost their sense of community and their sense of trust. Many are loners who have nothing to do with their neighbors, have no other family nearby, and have no real friends with whom they can discuss their problems. In some cases, living in a country place, far from other people, seems to play a part in child abuse.

People who hurt their children again and again are apt to have a poor opinion of themselves, to feel that they have failed in most everything they have tried, and to feel that they have little to offer the world. Perhaps as a result of this they expect too much of their children. If they have not been successful, they hope that their children will be winners and make them proud. They want to enjoy the reflected glory of their children's success, so they push the children very hard, often beyond what they can do. Parents treat these children as if they were older than they really are.

In some cases, parents really don't know what can be expected of children at various ages. June was a six-week-old baby when her father decided she should learn not to cry when he wanted her to be quiet. He punished her by spanking her when she did not stop crying. The more he hit her, the more she cried. In a fit of temper, he broke her ribs.

Many parents who were unloved or felt unloved as children look to their youngsters as a source of comfort and loving response. They act like children themselves and seem to consider their children as adults. They try to gain a parent when they have a child. This is known as "role reversal." Since the child cannot succeed in the impossible role of an adult, the parent feels rejected again.

Feelings of dependence, rage, and depression are acted out in beatings or other kinds of mistreatment.

Most parents have high hopes for their children as they look to the future. When parents hurt children who do not live up to their hopes, they are expecting the children to act like adults long before reaching that period in life. Part of this may be due to feelings of hate toward the parent's own past that alters understanding of the children's limited abilities and helplessness. What happens is twisted by the parent's own past experiences.

Sometimes fantasy in the form of role reversal takes place at the time of an attack on a child. A parent may imagine that the child is a nagging, critical mother or father from long ago. This parent, who does not know how to express feelings safely, strikes out at the child.

In most cases of role reversal, the parent was never able to secure love and support from his or her own parents or from other human beings during childhood. Lauren's case shows this.

Lauren brought her five-week-old baby to the hospital with bruises on his face. She explained that she had hit the baby because he did not love her. No one had ever loved her, and she had waited a long time for a baby who would. When the baby cried, she felt that he did not love her, so she hit him each time he cried.

Some parents are just not interested in their children. They may be especially irritated by a child who cries a great deal, or they may have very little patience. A television producer may lash out at a child who interferes with the work he brought home to meet an important schedule. He has no interest in any children, least of all his own child, who always seems to be demanding time he needs for his career.

One trait that many child abusers share is an inability to act in a manner appropriate to the seriousness of a problem. They strike out at children to relieve unbearable pressures. Whether the parents are rich or poor, the stress brings out any weaknesses in their personalities.

Bertha is a parent under stress. She works all day as a maid in a house where there is every comfort. At home, she makes dinner for her five children in a kitchen that has no counter space and no hot water. She tries to keep the house clean and neat, but there are no closets, and everything always seems to be all over the place. The children have a hard time understanding poverty. They want the things they see advertised on the old TV set that someone gave their mother. They cannot understand why she will not buy them.

One of Bertha's children is especially troublesome. Bertha watches him as he leans out the window. She feels like pushing him out. When he picks up her favorite ashtray and throws it out the window at a passing dog, Bertha hits him with a chair.

Bertha is sorry she hit her son, but she has just suffered too much this day. It is more than she can bear. She has always been too proud to ask for help, since she thinks that that means she is weak. She is overwhelmed with being a parent, and now she is a child abuser. The stress is just too much.

Confusion between discipline and abuse is a problem for some parents. Many people have a fear of spoiling a child or believe that one should not give in to children.

John's father was careful to show him who was boss. He told his friends that John was not going to be allowed to get away with some things the way other children could. He would be a strong parent. While he was trying to discipline John, his actions sometimes got out of hand and he would hurt the boy more than he meant to. When John upset his father's beer two times in one afternoon, the father exploded with anger. The only way to teach this clumsy child was to beat him, and even then he never seemed to learn. His father beat John until three ribs were broken.

Most abusing parents love their children and feel very upset when they discover that they have done something harmful. But they continue to lash out at their children when they feel that they are not getting anywhere with their attempts at discipline.

This is especially true when a parent does not know what to expect from a child at various ages.

Tim was only sixteen months old when his mother took him to the hospital because he had a "sore ear." When asked how the injury had happened, she explained that she was teaching Tim to come when he was called. When he did not obey, she tugged gently on his ear to remind him that he was supposed to do what she told him. Doctors at the hospital found that the ear was partly torn away from the child's head.

who

While some people who study the problem feel that there is more child abuse among poor people than among others, many disagree. They claim that the lives of poor people are more exposed to individuals who notice abuse. For example, welfare workers, social workers, day-care workers, and others see more poor children under school age than children of the middle and wealthy classes. People who can afford private help for their problems may never be included in the reports. Yet many poor people do suffer from more stress just in order to survive. No one really knows the truth in this argument, but one thing is certain—in all kinds of social situations, there are children in some families who suffer from abuse.

One of the most common characteristics of people who abuse their children is believed to be their own abuse when they were young. Much of how one behaves as a parent is learned from how one was treated as a child. This is why we often hear the expression "the cycle of abuse." Children who have been hurt are apt to hurt their own children, and when these children grow up they may continue the pattern. However, not all people who have been abused continue this kind of parenting.

The causes of abuse are many. New approaches to helping children who are mistreated and neglected include help for parents, too. Many doctors who see severely battered children try to understand why a parent has treated a child in such an ugly way. They must also consider whether or not it is safe to let the healed child go home with these parents. Getting the parents to accept help with their problems so the child will not continue to be abused is part of the healing process.

 Many people who abuse their children see life as something done to them rather than something they can manage. Things may be terrible for them, but they are resigned to it. "That's the way life is" is a common expression among people who do not know how to cope. But while they accept life as it is, they have difficulty controlling their anger and rage.

Most parents engage in some form of abuse at least one time in their lives, but this does not mean that they are abusive parents. If hurting a child is repeated and becomes a pattern of behavior, the parent has an abuse problem. Certainly, there are many forms of abuse and many different kinds of parents who abuse their children.

While child abusers may have many characteristics in common, there are only two that all of them share: they hurt their children, and they need help.

3

Who Are
the Crying Children?

Some children in a family are more likely to be mistreated than others, and often no one knows exactly why. Where one of the parents is a child abuser, it usually happens that only one child of two or more is the one to suffer. This special child is the one the parent sees as different from the others.

Actually, the child may indeed be different. He or she may have a birth defect, may be retarded, may be particularly active, may have a speech problem, may look like a hated relative, or have any of a wide variety of traits that peg a child as different. Sometimes the child is not the sex that the parents wanted. Or the child may have red hair instead of the blond hair they consider nicer.

Jim was the fifth child in a family of easygoing children. His temperament was different. Even during the first five weeks, his mother found that he hated new things. When she bathed him, an especially happy time for her other children, Jim screamed. He never cried softly, he always screamed. Jim was a "bad" baby. When his mother was under stress, she blamed all her problems on Jim. He was the child who took the verbal abuse.

Jim and other abused children are often the victims of problems that are not related to them, but they are chosen, rather than brothers and sisters, for some reason that makes them special.

Some children seem like little adults because they learn to fill their parents' needs for love and comfort at an early age. They take care of the parents instead of the parents taking care of them. Such a child develops a tendency to yield to others, a kind of behavior that is not usual for children. This boy or girl is deprived of a normal childhood. Also, he or she learns never to trust anyone. No one provides comfort or satisfies the child's need to feel safe.

In one family, a four-year-old child is always alert for the cries of her eighteen-month-old sister. She feeds her, comforts her when she cries, and takes her along wherever she goes. The four-year-old gets no positive feelings from her abusive mother, but she does develop some self-esteem through her care of her younger sister. This is at the expense of her own normal childhood and of her emotional health when she becomes an adult.

Paul has an unhappy situation at home. His mother is especially upset by any criticism, a long-standing condition that goes back to her childhood, when her own father rejected her. She fears being rejected by all men, and she has been unable to form a good relationship with her husband. She uses Paul as a substitute man around the house. He takes care of his younger brothers and sisters, helps his mother buy food, and cooks. When his mother goes out in the evenings, Paul goes with her in place of his father. His mother needs to depend on him so much that he is not permitted his own need to be dependent. He may well grow up to be an abusing parent. Deprived of the care he needed when he was young, he may never be able to provide it for others.

Betty is a seven-year-old who is withdrawn, underweight, and unlikable. She cannot get along with her classmates, since she is unwilling to take part in any activities in which she cannot be the boss. At home, Betty takes care of her mother, even feeding her when the mother says she is sick. Betty hoards food from the school lunch that is provided for her and takes it home to her mother. She knows that she will be asked the same question each day as soon as she gets home: "What did you bring me?" If Betty does not think of her mother before she thinks of herself, she is made to feel guilty. She is abused.

Twelve-year-old Sally was always afraid of her mother, a woman who would beat her with a belt that had a buckle on it. Sally did whatever her mother told her to do. She cared for her five younger brothers and sisters, staying home from school to take care of the little ones while her mother slept till noon. Sally did not enjoy her role as mother. In fact, she teased the children and was sullen and depressed. She ate a great deal and was quite fat. Much of her anger was turned against herself, but she could not escape from the hold her mother had on her.

Even when children are very young, signs of mistreatment can often be detected by a person who knows what to look for. For example, when most babies are brought to a doctor's office and placed on an examining table, they turn toward their mothers. An abused baby does not. This baby is usually fearful of being touched by any adult and may cry hopelessly while being examined. There is little or no eye contact between the parent and the baby. An abused child may appear to be alert for danger at a very young age.

When young children who have been battered are placed in a hospital, most of them do not ask to go home the way other children do. They are wary of being touched by adults and seem always to wonder what is coming next. Usually children in a hospital become interested in other children in a ward and reach out to adults for help after a short time. While some seem unafraid of being in a ward and settle in unusually fast, others exhibit "frozen watchfulness." This has been seen in children as young as nine or ten months. These abused children tend to sit or lie still, watching quietly whatever is going on around them. They may remain quietly alert for several days, watching to see what is going to happen. Others ask again and again, "What is going to happen next?"

When abused children reach school age, teachers may recognize them from one or more of the following clues. These are not proof of maltreatment, since they can reflect other situations, but they are danger signs:

> Coming to school with dirty clothing, body odor, or unkempt appearance
> Having unexplained injury
> Acting shy, withdrawn, or too eager to cooperate
> Arriving at school early and leaving late
> Not wanting to go home
> Wearing long-sleeved clothes in warm weather
> Talking about beatings
> Acting nervous, too active, or destructive
> Acting fearful of being touched by an adult
> Being absent from school with poor or no excuses
> Showing little hope of being comforted when in trouble
> Always searching for favors, food, or services

Having problems in getting along with other children

No one of these is necessarily a sign of abuse at home, but a child showing several of these clues may make a teacher suspicious. An abused child is a lonely, joyless person who has little contact with people of his or her own age. You, alone, may not be able to identify an abused child, but your teacher may be alerted to recognize clues if you talk about them.

Children who are old enough to talk often deny that they have been abused, either because they feel a loyalty to their parents or because they fear they will be further abused for telling. Since they do not usually trust others, these children keep the secrets in the family.

Trina is an abused child whose case is well known because it was described in an article in *Life* magazine. This thirteen-year-old girl claimed she murdered a fourteen-year-old girl because of jealousy. Since Trina gave a number of different accounts of the murder, skilled investigators were confused about whether or not she was really guilty. Actually, the confession was a plea for help by an abused child.

Trina's life was lonely and loveless. Her mother was an alcoholic who could not cope with her own problems. Trina tried to get attention from her mother in a number of ways, but it was no use. When her mother went through a religious conversion and stopped drinking, the relationship between mother and daughter remained difficult.

Trina did not remember the last time she saw her real father, the second of her mother's five husbands. After studying her case, psychologists concluded that Trina's life was so ugly that she became a chronic liar. So it was not difficult for her to lie about a murder she did not commit.

Trina was clever in the way she confessed the murder. By memorizing facts that she read in newspapers and by gathering information from the detectives who interviewed her, Trina was able to fool the investigators. Trina claimed this was not difficult since the investigators often suggested what happened and then asked if that was right.

After her confession, Trina was placed in detention by the police, a place she preferred to home. At least she was not being beaten. In a sense she had been in jail at home during the month before she confessed to the murder. She had spent some time confined to a small bedroom where the window was covered and bolted shut in an effort to keep her from seeing a boy with whom she had become sexually involved. Although her mother was quick to express concern about Trina's affair in this strange way, she had refused to believe Trina's earlier complaints that she had been sexually molested until one of the offenders admitted it.

Shortly before the murder confession, Trina began to feel that she could do nothing right. Her mother was very discouraged with her behavior, and by the time she confessed to the murder, her mother actually considered her capable of it.

It took two months before the case against Trina was dismantled. During this period, Trina made it clear that she craved affection and that she wanted to be important. She cooperated with the police and admitted that she hoped they would like her.

Trina was removed from her home and given intensive therapy. But what a tragedy it is that an abused child should have to go to such lengths in order to get help.

Many foster children suffer from the abuse of moving from home to home before they can settle into a good relationship with their foster parents, even if they are lucky enough to be placed with caring people. Many of these children are difficult because of the abuse that began with their own parents. Reggie is an example of such a case. He was severely punished by his mother for a variety of offenses, some of them real and some of them imaginary. After his mother's boyfriend threw him out of a second-story window, he spent some time in the hospital recovering from a broken wrist and spinal injuries. While he was there, social workers classed him as a neglected child and placed him in the foster-care system. He lived in a series of group homes. At one point, Reggie had a foster mother who really cared about him. But when she went on an extended vacation, Reggie was placed in another foster home and then in several group homes.

Many children in the foster-care system suffer from a system that is overcrowded. There are not enough homes for them and not enough social workers to give them the help they need. Foster care is meant to be temporary care, but the average length of stay in the New York area is four years. Many children, for a variety of reasons, never return to the homes from which they originally came.

Some children who are abused at home try to solve their problems by running away and living in the streets. They sleep on subways, in waiting rooms, and in deserted buildings. They eat food they steal from stores and scavenge from trash cans. Many become prostitutes in order to survive.

Abused children can be found anywhere, but some children, such as those in foster care, are more at risk than others. John H. Meier, a well-known authority on child abuse and Director of the Research Division of Childhelp USA/International, lists the following factors that put a child at risk: being an unwanted child; being a problem child (colicky, incontinent, physically or emotionally ill, deformed, or developmentally disabled);

behaving provocatively (hyperactive, a discipline problem, whining, jealous of siblings, sexually acting-out, dishonest, amoral, swearing, throwing tantrums, destroying possessions, unresponsive, withdrawn, uncommunicative, or subject to such stress/anxiety factors as a failed grade, being a bully's victim, and so forth). For parents under stress and those who have not learned good parenting skills, any of the above characteristics are contributing factors for abuse.

Many young mothers, who themselves are adolescents still in need of some mothering, do not have the physical, financial, and psychic resources to deal with the needs of newborn children. The additional burden of a child, especially one with one or more of the above problems, puts the baby at risk of abuse.

Even though the victim of child abuse is often the child of a parent who was abused, many children are able to break out of the vicious cycle. Not all children who are abused grow up to be abusers. Although there is no panacea in sight, new approaches are helping to break the cycle and prevent abuse of today's children.

Learning about who is at risk is an important step in prevention. In the National Study of Child Neglect and Abuse Report, a research effort by the American Humane Association's Child Protection Division, an attempt was made to record all reported cases of child abuse and neglect since the year 1973. In addition to this, a major research effort for the federal government's National Center on Child Abuse and Neglect attempted to provide information about numbers and characteristics of maltreated children beyond those provided through official reports. The results of this research provide some insight into the "average" troubled family.

The average age of children reported in one year as abused and/or neglected was seven and one half years. Preschool children, from birth to five years of age, represented 28 percent of the overall child population but accounted for 74 percent of maltreatment fatalities.

Generally, the incidence rate for maltreatment increases with age with two exceptions: (1) the physical neglect of both boys and girls is relatively constant and similar for all age groups over two years; (2) the physical abuse of boys decreases after age five.

The incidence rate for sexual abuse is highest among adolescent females, but half the female victims of sexual abuse are under eleven years of age.

No geographic setting is free of child abuse and neglect. The incidence rates are similar for urban, suburban, and rural communities, but the type of abuse differs. For example, in rural counties the incidence rate for sexual abuse is higher than elsewhere. In urban areas the incidence rate for educational neglect is higher than elsewhere. In suburban locations the incidence rate for emotional neglect is higher than elsewhere.

Although there is no way to determine the true number of children who suffer from child abuse, one thing is certain. The number is large. If we think in terms of these large numbers, abuse may seem less real. If we consider the death of one battered child, it becomes a tragedy.

4
Children
of Very Long Ago

Child abuse is not new. If you lived long ago, your chances of being hurt would have been much greater than they are today. Infanticide, the killing of young babies, was a widely accepted practice in many parts of the world. Infanticide, in olden times, was not considered murder because it was killing with consent of the parent, family, or community. In some cases, the reason was simply not enough food for a large family. In some cultures, any child born after the third was either killed or eliminated by being sold or abandoned.

Children born out of wedlock were often the victims of infanticide because of dishonor, poor care, or the economic plight of the mother. Many illegitimate babies were abandoned. Since the infant almost always died, this usually amounted to infanticide. Some infants were placed in the care of nurses, who collected a fee and then did away with the babies. Many children were kept to be used for begging on the streets for money they had to turn over to the adults.

Sacrificing a child to the gods was common in ancient times. The case of Abraham, who offered his son Isaac as a sacrifice but whose hand was stayed by divine intervention, is better known and has a happier ending than most cases. In some cultures, the firstborn son was always sacrificed, while in others the firstborn son was allowed to live but other sons were not. This prevented problems about who would inherit the family's possessions.

Children who were weak, had birth defects, were girls, or were unwanted for some other reason were put to death soon after birth. If you think about the reasons for infanticide, you will not find it difficult to believe that babies were not valued long ago as they are in today's world. Although mothers occasionally dispose of their children today, these are punishable as serious crimes.

Were there other kinds of abuse in times gone by? How were the children who lived treated in early times? One hopes that many of them were loved, but records show that it was not uncommon for parents to abandon an infant. Through the centuries, many children were left on mountainsides where wild animals would find them, in rivers where they would drown, or in any nearby place where they would starve to death or become victims of the elements. As late as the eighteenth century in England, children were left in the streets to die while people walked by with little or no concern. For centuries, many children died at an early age. One reason for widespread child abuse is thought to be the lack of feeling for a child who would probably never live to grow up. Perhaps parents were afraid to become attached to children. If they did not care about them, they would not suffer when the children were lost.

Another factor in child abuse was the parent-child relationship. In general, the lot of boys and girls throughout history was a hard one. From one era to the next, generation after generation, the child was the property of the father to do with as he wished. This was written into law in the Code of Hammurabi, which was based on early Babylonian law, dating back to 2130 B.C. According to the code, a man was free to give his child (or wife) in payment of a debt. The child could be sold or exchanged for goods. In days gone by, being sold into slavery was a form of abuse many children had to endure.

Codes that followed this earliest set of laws included similar powers for fathers. The child was the property of the father, who was entitled to absolute respect. While children made out somewhat better during the height of Greek civilization, about five hundred years before the birth of Christ, these attitudes later disappeared.

Even in early Greece, fathers would decide whether a baby would be allowed to live or die. In the upper classes, the child was laid at the father's feet soon after birth. If he picked it up, the child was accepted and allowed to live, but if he turned away, a slave disposed of the child by placing it in a large jar or throwing it into a manure heap or a river. Aristotle wrote that "the justice of a master or a father is a different thing from that of a citizen, for a son or slave is property, and there can be no injustice to one's own property."

Sometimes, babies were left where people would see them, with the hope that they would be adopted. A precious stone or something of value might be tied to the baby, perhaps to make a person who saw it believe that adoption would bring good luck. Child abuse was often the next thing in store for these babies. Adults plucked out their eyes, twisted their legs, or cut off their hands and feet and sent them, as little children, out to beg. Young beggars who were deformed caused both pity and amusement in some adults in ancient times. Attitudes about children have changed so much since then that today it is difficult to imagine deliberately harming a child for the sake of a few more pennies.

Through the years, people paid no attention to

the mistreatment and suffering of children. This was true of people who saw the children, of people who knew them, and, in many cases, of their parents. Some children were treated with love and kindness, but this attention was often at the whim of the parents. Everyone was used to seeing children abused. This was the custom for many years. This was the way life was. Survival was difficult for most adults, and little attempt was made to soften life for children.

Much indifference and cruelty to children was probably caused by ignorance of the conditions necessary for their well-being. Superstitions were the basis of much that passed for care. A child who was born under a curse carried that curse for a lifetime.

In much of the period known as the Middle Ages (roughly A.D. 500–1500), children continued to suffer. In some houses, children slept on the floor with domestic animals. They shared the dirt, the worms, and the diseases. People did not consider this child abuse, for no one knew any better. Children of wealthy parents slept on the floor of the great hall with the servants, and all of them were considered on a level with servants.

Poor children worked along with their parents when they were barely more than infants. All children worked for the manor or the community beginning at an early age. Family life, in which a mother, father, and children were a unit, was not known until the seventeenth century.

It was common for children over seven to learn through serving a family other than their own in what was known as apprenticeship. This was also called "binding out." The arrangement was made by the father, who decided where to place the child and for how long. Children had no choice in the matter. Children of rich people were usually sent to another castle or to a church. Middle-class boys were sent to craftsmen to do their menial tasks and to learn from them, and girls were sent to other households to act as servants. Poor children either were kept with their parents, helping them with the chores necessary for their survival, or were placed in the lowest kind of service.

No matter how they were treated, apprentices were forced to work under the arrangements made by their parents. Many children were severely beaten, and probably few escaped what would be considered severe abuse in today's world.

Children were plentiful, even though many died at an early age. According to some theories, parents considered children easier to replace than their more expensive domestic animals. This was true even though only one in two or three lived through childhood. Spoiled food, fire, and famine took their toll, along with epidemics of plague, influenza, smallpox, tuberculosis, dysentery, and typhoid.

Adults, too, suffered from these diseases, and many children were orphaned at birth or in their early years. Groups of little boys and girls were put in the care of women, who treated them in any way they wished. Few of these women, if any, spared the rod. Beatings were common.

During most of the Middle Ages, parents continued to neglect their children. The little attention children did receive was often a form of physical abuse. But toward the end of the Middle Ages, in the twelfth and thirteenth centuries, the status of children improved somewhat. This was partly due to the growth of chivalry and partly due to an interest in the infant Jesus. In the past, Christians had not thought of him as a typical child, but around this period, they thought of the young Jesus as having more human qualities. Children in general were better off because of this interest.

But child abuse did not disappear. This was especially true in the case of children of the poor and children who were orphaned or disowned. Poor families continued to struggle for survival, their children working side by side with the adults at a very early age.

Beatings were still common for children in all classes. Even King Henry VI was flogged regularly by his tutor when he was growing up. Charles I was more fortunate, since he had a whipping boy who took his beatings. Even though some adults spoke up against harsh physical abuse, children continued to be whipped. There are accounts of battered children who died as a result of beatings, but most cases probably went unnoticed.

5

Hurt Children
in Yesterday's England

Early English law of about A.D. 1300 was similar to Roman law in the treatment of children. A father had complete control over the young, and in times of poverty he could sell a son or a daughter. A child could own property at this time in England and the father acted as guardian until a certain age was reached. A few hundred years later, the old Roman idea that the state could take over the duties of parents was adopted in England. These English laws and those that followed were the basis of laws in the United States.

By the sixteenth century in England, the number of poor people was so great that large numbers were starving. Many parents and their children had to beg for enough food to keep them alive. The Poor Relief Act of 1601 was passed to make work for those children whose parents could not provide for them. As a result of these so-called poor laws, children whose parents could not feed them were taken from them permanently. The laws did not work very well, and about fifty years later, the government of England used another system that placed children in workhouses for the poor.

Conditions in the workhouses were so bad that almost all the children sent there died. For babies less than one year old the death rate was 99 percent, and for those slightly older it was 80 percent to 90 percent. A child's chances of survival, no matter where, were still poor. Even though the family—mother, father, and children—had evolved as a unit and parents showed more concern for their children than before, many children still died before the age of five. Abuse of all sorts was still common.

The great gin-drinking period of London in the eighteenth century was one of tragedy and horror. Gin was cheap and brought forgetfulness of cold and misery. One famous case of child abuse of the time was recorded in the Sessions Papers of Old Bailey (the jail) of 1734. Judith Dufour took her two-year-old child from the workhouse where it had just been newly clothed. She pretended to take it out for the afternoon, but she strangled the child and left it in a ditch after removing the clothing. She sold the clothing for money, which she and a friend used to buy gin. Judith Dufour worked all that night in a mill, and there she confessed what she had done to another woman who worked with her. She was accused of the crime and probably punished, but many other child abusers were never recognized.

The children who were exposed in the streets of London had long been a problem for some people who had developed feelings of social concern. These people worked for years to establish the London Foundling Hospital. In 1739, the following was signed by a number of ladies of rank and presented to the government:

> No expedient has yet been found out for preventing the murder of poor miserable infants at their birth, or suppressing the inhuman custom of exposing newly-born infants to perish in the streets; or the putting of such unhappy foundlings to wicked and barbarous nurses, who undertake to bring them up for a small and trifling sum of money, do often suffer them to starve for want of due sustenance or care, or if permitted to live . . . turn them into the streets to beg or steal.

The London Foundling Hospital was established, but it could care for only a limited number of children. Further work on the part of interested and charitable people improved the lot of poor children to some degree, but there was still a great deal of hardship and cruelty.

For hundreds of years, the hours that children

worked on the farms remained about the same. In winter, they worked from dawn to dusk, and in the spring from eight to six. In harvesttime, many worked from five in the morning until nine at night. For this work, the reward was small, but it added to the wages of the fathers and mothers. Children were put to work as soon as they were able to earn money, and no one saw any abuse in this way of adding to the family income.

The children who were sent to school were disciplined by flogging there as well as at home. Parents took seriously the Bible warning, "Spare the rod and spoil the child." Many parents truly believed that giving harsh beatings was part of their responsibility in raising a child. But here and there a voice was raised in defense of children, and for some children life was less harsh.

Jean-Jacques Rousseau, a Frenchman, played an important part in changing attitudes about children. He recognized that there were definite periods of development in a child's life, and that a child was not just a miniature adult. But in spite of his enlightened attitude, Rousseau abandoned his own children. However, his book *Émile,* published in 1762, had an important influence on child care in England. For some children, their recognition as persons meant less abuse, but this was not true for all children.

When making goods took place in homes, children helped with the chores, working long hours in cottage industries such as spinning and weaving. In the middle of the eighteenth century, around the time that George Washington was growing up in America, it was not uncommon to find English children of the ages of three and four working in the factories. Little children picked up the waste cotton from the floors. They were especially valuable as workers who could creep under the machines where older and larger people could not go.

Older children suffered a different kind of abuse. They were made to work fifteen hours a day, sometimes at night. If they refused, they were beaten. Large numbers of children worked under the pressure of this fear.

The harshness of many parents in eighteenth-century England fills today's students of the times with horror. The laws were equally cruel. Children were not exempt from being publicly hanged, and in some cases the offense was trivial. For example, a little girl seven years of age was hanged in the marketplace for stealing a petticoat. Parents considered it good discipline to take their children to see the body of a murderer hanging in chains.

Jonas Hanway, who was active in protecting youngsters, protested against the abuse of children who were put to work sweeping chimneys. His concern for them is easily understood when one reads about their lot in life.

Jeff was a climbing-boy for a chimney sweep in London about two hundred years ago. He was one of many young boys who were sold or abandoned at a very young age. Jeff was told to climb up a chimney of the local church, but the area was small and he had to struggle to get into the space. His master, the sweep, sent another boy to poke him by putting his head underneath Jeff's body. At other times, during a period of two hours, Jeff was pricked by a pin fastened to the end of a stick. One time when he tried to come down, a small fire was built under him. He cleaned the chimney as best he could, but the skin was rubbed from his knees and elbows. He had perspired so much from both fear and exertion while trying to clean the chimney that his body was covered with sweat, much as if water had been thrown on him.

This actual case was reported in *The Lady's Magazine, An Entertaining Companion for the Fair Sex* (vol. 43), in London, December 31, 1802. Many similar reports could be made, for it was well known that climbing-boys were physically abused just by the nature of their work. Not until 1788 was a bill passed in Parliament that prohibited boys under the age of eight from becoming apprentices and forbidding a sweep from having more than six boys at one time. Unfortunately for the boys, the act was almost totally ignored.

In the year 1800, the Society for Superseding the

Necessity of Climbing-Boys was formed. This group tried to encourage the use of a special kind of brush that was invented at that time. But this and similar brushes were not commonly used until nearly a hundred years later.

Climbing-boys often became deformed from their work, and many who worked in the soot developed cancer. A report published at the time claimed that those who survived "came to no good." Many children were overcome by fumes and some suffocated in the chimney flues. Common treatment for the inevitable bleeding knees and elbows consisted of rubbing them with salt water to harden the raw flesh.

Children were abused in a variety of work situations. During the eighteenth and nineteenth centuries, many children were employed in the mines, where they worked for twelve hours a day. Some of the little ones were trappers, who opened and shut the trapdoors that controlled the ventilation of the mines. Children also filled carriages with coal and pushed the trucks from the end of the tunnel to the shaft of the mine, where the coal could be raised to the surface.

If you had lived at the time of Sarah Gooder, who was eight years old in 1842, you might not have thought about her situation the way you do today. But even by the standards of the time, she was considered abused by some people who took the trouble to care. Sarah described her day as a trapper in the pit of a mine, where she worked from four in the morning until half past five at night. She was scared in the dark. She said that she sometimes sang when she saw the daylight. She could not sing in the dark because of her fear. Sarah claimed that she never went to sleep.

Sarah's story, and the stories of other girls who drew trucks along the paths in the coal mines, was presented to the English Parliament in 1842 and resulted in a ruling against the employment of children under ten in the mines.

In the eighteenth century, apprenticeship was still the way of giving children a start in life while using their work to pay for their keep. In the case of poor children, the fee received for apprenticeship was low. Masters and mistresses might be "tigers in cruelty." They might beat, abuse, strip naked, starve, or do what they wished with an innocent child. No one would notice.

Children were bound out, or apprenticed, to be domestic servants, were kidnapped or sent by parents to be members of gangs who worked long hours on plantations, were sent into the streets to hawk milk, and were apprenticed in a wide variety of ways.

The poor laws of the time forced a parish or community to pay the apprentice fee for a poor child. Placing children in another parish got rid of the obligation. In most cases, no one cared to whom or for what kind of work a child was apprenticed as long as the master or mistress lived in another parish. There were those who secured the fee for taking an apprentice and then got rid of the child by such cruel treatment that child ran away.

By the nineteenth century a new phase in the protection of children had begun. The movement gathered the support of many people. Certainly, child abuse was not a problem just for poor children, although they may have been victims more often. In the crusade to protect children, a "lady of position" named Mrs. Montague was convicted of manslaughter in the year 1892. She had tied up her small daughter and locked her in a cupboard for five hours. The child died. It was argued in her defense that a parent had a right to punish a child in a reasonable manner, but she was sentenced to twelve months' imprisonment.

Through the years, societies for the prevention of cruelty to children were formed in England. Prosecutions of caretakers, including parents, for neglect and cruelty to children became more frequent. People were coming to understand and appreciate the conditions necessary for human life and to realize that children are persons, not property.

The Children Act of 1948 is considered an important law, not only because it brought together

the administration of child care into a single service, but because of the idea of children's rights on
which the service was based. Now it was openly
agreed that all children, rich and poor alike, had
the rights of support, security, health, happiness,
and fulfillment. This was not the end of all child
abuse, but it was a long way from conditions of
even a hundred years earlier.

6

Child Abuse: American Style

While American children generally had more freedom than those in England, child labor followed the colonists to America. The Puritans considered the work experience a proper way to train a child. Apprenticeship was practiced in colonial days, and many children were bound out to service when they were as young as four years of age.

There are records of cases in which abuse was considered serious enough to be brought to court. In Salem, Massachusetts, in the year 1630, a man was brought to trial for murdering his apprentice, but he was acquitted by a jury because they considered that the boy was "ill disposed." The jury did find the boy's punishment to be unreasonable, since it evidently caused the boy's skull to be broken. In another case, a man who killed his apprentice through a series of beatings was said to have been executed in Boston, Massachusetts, in the year

1643. Perhaps the difference between these two cases was the fact that the first incident of abuse was not part of a pattern. No one knows how many young apprentices were treated kindly or how many were abused by beatings. Probably a great many children worked for very long hours.

According to custom, many children of colonial times were severely punished when they did not obey. The Stubborn Child Law, which was passed in Massachusetts in the year 1646, called for the death of children who were not obedient, providing their parents were not at fault. Public whipping was usually substituted, but there was no doubt about the rights of parents to force their wishes on their children. The Stubborn Child Law was finally repealed in 1973.

Parents had the right to any money that their children earned, and money earned by any children they chose to accept into their families. Many British children were shipped to the colonies and put to work under contract, but they received no wages other than their keep.

Through the centuries, some voices were raised against the plight of children who worked in factories from the time they were very young. It was pointed out that they had little chance for fresh air, play, or education. Laws were passed to protect children, but, as in England, they were not strictly enforced. Many children who suffered the abuse of long hours and poor pay grew up in poverty, untrained for anything better than the unskilled work they did for long hours as children.

Child labor was accepted by the public as a service to the poor, a way for children to help support their families. Hard work was considered a good thing, and the old saying that hard work never hurt anyone was applied without serious thought to children as well as to adults.

Abandoned children who were too young or too sick to work were taken to almshouses, where they were assigned to the care of the poor women who were living there. As in England, conditions at the almshouses were horrid, and many of the babies who were sent there died at a very young age. Children were housed with the disabled and diseased in dirty conditions and given no education. Babies were supposed to be fed by wet nurses, women whose breasts had recently supplied milk for their own babies. These wet nurses were so much in demand that some abandoned children were sent out to live with families. Conditions in these homes were no better than in the almshouses.

During the period that followed the Civil War, times were especially bad. In New York City, there were so many babies abandoned on doorsteps, left in gutters, and thrown in trash cans that the Sisters of Charity received support in their efforts to help children. Sister Mary Irene Fitzgibbon and two other nuns opened the door of a small house to abandoned babies. This was the beginning of the New York Foundling Hospital. On October 11, 1869, the Sisters placed a small crib at the entrance to the house and let it be known through the city's newspapers that they would care for any unwanted infants who were placed there.

In the days and months that followed, the little crib was seldom empty. Some children were left with notes pinned to their clothing telling their names. Some were dressed in rags and some in fine clothes. A dollar or two was often found along, with a baby, and a note that said the mother had no more money to care for the child. Over a thousand babies were received during the first year, but at least as many were discarded in the streets over a two-year period. The New York Foundling Hospital continued to grow through the years, and it still provides help for a limited number of neglected and abused children as well as for their parents.

Since the attitude toward children in the nineteenth century continued to be one that upheld the rights of parents to punish their children as they wished, many children were cruelly treated by their parents. They had no protection under the law, but a step toward their protection was made in 1838. In that year, the Supreme Court of Pennsylvania reached the decision that the state government could, in some cases, rule to take children from parents who did not or would not care for them. This made the state government guardian of these children, as in England.

What would happen to the wards of the state? During the last century in America, many reform schools, farm schools, orphanages, and asylums of various kinds sprang into being. Children who broke the law, children who were abandoned or neglected, and children who were orphaned were housed in them. By the turn of the century there was a vast network of orphan asylums, but many orphans were still found with juvenile and adult offenders. In many cases the neglected became the abused, and those who were not "wayward" learned from those who were living in the institutions because they had broken the law. Many children who had already suffered from abuse at home were now at the mercy of guards who used harsh discipline.

By the year 1845, some of the children who had been in orphanages and other institutions were placed in foster homes. Large numbers of children went to work for farmers, who took them into their families. In many cases, this worked out very well. But even after the slaves were freed by the Civil War, children in all parts of the country were still put to work on the farms at a very young age and made to work in the fields from sunrise to sunset. Other children worked long hours in mines, in mills, and in factories. Even those who received some schooling were "taught to the tune of a hickory stick."

Between the years 1854 and 1875, about twenty thousand children were sent to the West to find new homes with any family who befriended them. Groups of boys and girls arrived at a destination by train and were taken to a meeting where a large crowd had gathered. The children were set apart from the group one by one, while a leader read a brief account of each child. An applicant from the crowd selected a child, the child nodded assent, and the agreement was sealed. It is hard to imagine such a child, tired from the trip and confused by strange surroundings, refusing anyone who promised a home. No one checked to find out whether or not each home was a good one, so no one knows how many children were loved and how many were abused.

About this time, orphanages placed older children with families as a way of disposing of them rather than as a part of a supervised child care program. Even homes nearby were not investigated, and no one followed a case to see what was happening. Many people encouraged the placement of children in foster homes to get them away from the cold and strict life in most orphanages. Unfortunately, the careless placement of children in these years gave foster care a bad name. As a result, many children were held in institutions for all of their childhood.

While some orphanages may have been good places to live, most were believed to be highly rigid. The children who lived there had little chance of developing the characteristics they needed to deal with the problems of adult life. Through the years, standards of placement for foster care were developed and there was supervision by social agencies, but this process developed slowly. One reason was that there were never enough funds to provide enough social workers.

One case of child abuse that is now famous made people more aware of the problem. In 1874, a nine-year-old girl named Mary Ellen was found chained to her bed in the home of the foster parents with whom she had been placed. Concerned neighbors in the poor, crowded section of New York City where the girl lived reported their suspicions of ill-treatment to a nurse who was in the area. The nurse discovered that the little girl was not only chained to the bedpost but was also underfed. Her body showed signs of having been beaten during different periods of her development. The nurse and some church workers told the police and the district attorney about Mary Ellen, but there was no law in New York to enable them to take her away from her foster parents. She was their property, and they could treat her as they wished.

On behalf of Mary Ellen, the nurse and the concerned church workers went to the Society for the Prevention of Cruelty to Animals for help. They pointed out that she was a member of the animal kingdom. The society had the right to remove animals from places where they were ill-treated, and on this basis they removed Mary Ellen from her home. She was taken to court on a stretcher because she was too weak to walk, but her life was saved because some people cared about her.

People who heard about Mary Ellen were shocked to realize that more was being done to protect animals from abuse than to protect children. This was partly due to the idea that no one dared invade the privacy of the home or contest the rights of parents. The Society for the Prevention of Cruelty to Children was soon organized in New York, and many other groups were formed to help abused and neglected children in other parts of the country. By the year 1900 there were 161 similar groups in the United States. This progress was only a beginning in the attempts to change the lot of victims of child abuse. Only a very small percentage of abused children were reached, and these were mostly cases of severe physical abuse in which children were legally removed from parents who were punished.

At the beginning of this century, millions of children were still working very long hours in mills, factories, and mines as well as on the farms. In the next ten to twenty years, laws were passed to protect young workers. The youngest age at which children could begin work was ten. This eventually was raised to sixteen years of age in many states. The introduction of laws requiring children to go to school also helped to reduce child labor.

Early in the twentieth century, people trying to prevent and treat child abuse began to change their approach from punishing parents to helping the family. In the 1930s, the Social Security Act made some funds available for the prevention and treatment of child abuse, with emphasis on children in rural areas where other welfare services were not available. The establishment of the Children's Bureau as part of a federal agency helped to provide child protection services throughout the country. A network of public and private agencies grew in efforts to provide services such as adoption, foster care, care in institutions, day care, supportive services, and protection from abuse. The Child Welfare League of America began its work, which included the setting of standards in many areas of child care.

Since children are still being abused in homes and in institutions, it is obvious that the labor and education laws and efforts to improve child welfare have not solved all the problems. For many years doctors in hospitals noticed that some young children had strange "accidents," leaving them with injuries that could not be explained.

In 1946, Dr. John Caffey studied the x-rays of many injured children and called attention to cases of infants with fractured bones that did not seem to be the result of accidents. At first he did not suggest that the parents could have been responsible, but later he did speak out about this possibility. However, child abuse was still a problem too unpleasant for many doctors to accept.

During the next fifteen years, other doctors concluded that many long-bone fractures and bruises on infants who were brought to the emergency rooms might have been caused by the action of parents. But no name was given to the problem until Dr. C. Henry Kempe expressed his concern about children he treated at the Colorado General Hospital. He became alarmed because many accidents could not be explained to his satisfaction. In just one day in November 1961 there were four children in the Colorado General Hospital who appeared to have been beaten. Two of the children died in the hospital and another died after being sent home. Dr. Kempe had observed so many cases of children who suffered from injuries that did not appear to be accidental that he suggested the term "battered child syndrome." He used this term to make people aware of what he had discovered when he contacted law officers and hospitals in various parts of the country. His work was responsible for much of the present interest in child abuse.

Even in 1968, when Dr. Kempe and Dr. Ray E. Helfer's book *The Battered Child* appeared, few people were aware of the amount of physical beating of children in the United States. This book was widely read by thousands upon thousands of people who were uninformed or who had shunned an unpleasant problem. People did not want to believe that parents would turn their anger on their own children, but an article on the battered child syndrome in a medical journal commanded the attention of doctors throughout the United States. It was no longer possible to deny the existence of child abuse.

New reporting laws were passed and experts began a new search into the true causes of child abuse. The search for causes and ways to prevent and treat child abuse continues.

Today, everyone can help to prevent the hurt.

7

Preventing
Child Abuse

Many children suffer every day because people, usually people they know, are abusing them sexually and physically. Just knowing that child abuse is the number one killer of young children is enough to make most people want to do something to help prevent it. When they realize that the abused children of today often become the juvenile delinquents and criminals of tomorrow, even the hardhearted are moved to action.

Many abused children develop learning problems and habits that destroy emotional and physical health. Many well-known criminals, including John Wilkes Booth, Lee Harvey Oswald, Arthur Bremmer, Sirhan Sirhan, and James Earl Ray, were abused as children. No one knows exactly how much child abuse contributes to crimes, but according to one study, 80 percent of the people who are sent to jails and prisons for serious crimes were abused or neglected as children. Criminals, alcoholics, and other drug addicts are a burden on society. Child abuse hurts everyone. The cost to society can never be fully counted. No wonder that people who care only about their taxes join people who are concerned for the lives of innocent children in asking, "What can I do?"

Until recently, it was common to avoid the problem by blaming the parents who abuse their children. If one considers parents to be the only ones responsible for their actions, it is easy to turn away. Today, there is more awareness of the big picture. While parents must bear part of the blame, experts see that society is responsible too. Under a certain combination of circumstances, anyone could abuse or neglect a child.

Many experts see child abuse as a problem of the powerful over the powerless. They compare it with society's failure to meet the needs of people who are emotionally ill, unemployed, mentally retarded, or discriminated against for other reasons. These people, whose self-esteem is usually low, may have great difficulty in holding others in high esteem, and these others include their own children. Parents with high self-esteem are more able to provide love and affection, while parents with low self-esteem are more likely to lash out at their children.

People may shy away from the problem of child abuse because they feel guilty about the plight of the powerless and the way society neglects them. For example, society allows or ignores terrible conditions in mental hospitals, people turn away from the problems of migrant workers, they ignore the problems of the elderly poor, and so forth. The person who abuses a child is only another example of the powerful doing bad things to the powerless. Since society and everyone in it is more or less responsible for these situations, some of the anger people feel for the abusing parent may be anger they feel for themselves. Many young people do not feel this anger, and young people may be the very ones who can play a big part in helping to prevent child abuse. They know that preventing child abuse is far more than reporting the tragic case of a single child, important as that may be. Young people can help to promote improved policies concerning health, unemployment, welfare, and other social issues that affect the quality of life of children. Young people can make adults aware of the hurt children who cry softly.

Certainly, children in the United States have come a long way in the two centuries since the American Revolution. Fewer boys and girls die from starvation and disease, fewer children labor for their keep, and almost all parents consider their children to have some rights. New agencies and laws help to protect the rights of children, but they do not reach them all.

The number of children who are abused is frighteningly large. Millions of children are in desperate trouble because they are experiencing severe and frequent violence in their homes. Millions more are suffering from forms of abuse other than physical.

Young people are helping to make the public aware of the extent of child abuse by their letters to newspapers, by spreading the word to adults and friends in conversations, and by getting the interest of groups who can persuade radio and television stations to carry short announcements on the subject. Organizations listed at the end of this book can provide ideas.

Suppose you read an article in the paper about an abused child. For example, *The New York Times* printed an account of a little girl about eight years old who was found about five blocks from her home at four o'clock in the morning. She was underfed, dressed in ragged clothing, and seemed deeply frightened. She would not, or could not, talk, and her muscles were in such poor condition that she could not walk. There were cigarette burns and belt marks on her body.

When the grandmother and the mother visited the girl in the hospital after recognizing her from a television report, she showed no sign of knowing them.

If it had not been for a phone call by a person who did not give a name, the little girl might not have been found. But someone reported the abused child and, in this way, made help available.

When you read an article like this, you will find that community interest is greater than at other times. Readers of the article will be more concerned about all child abuse, so it is a good time to write to your local newspaper about the problem. You might wish to call attention to these points:

Child abuse and neglect in the United States is a serious problem. Most people have no idea that it is one of the leading causes of death for children.

Both parents and children are the victims of child abuse. Punishing parents turns them away from seeking sources of help. Both children and parents need help.

About 90 percent of all child abuse is treatable. There are many ways in which parents can obtain help even without telling their names. (Suggestions are described in the next chapter.) Child abuse happens in all kinds of families.

These are just a few facts that can be included in a letter or a radio spot. You may wish to choose one idea and encourage groups to make posters that can spread the message in your community. Sometimes local printers will donate their services. Use short messages, such as CHILD ABUSE HURTS EVERYONE. Anyone can print this on a poster and tack it in a place where many people will see it.

One of the important ways to help prevent child abuse is supporting and encouraging research into the causes. What does the rooming-in of newborn babies with their mothers in hospitals have to do with child abuse prevention? The answer to this question is just one example of how research can help. In this case, rooming-in may help to break the cycle of child abuse as soon as babies are born.

Experiments show that parents and newborn infant feel intense emotion when they interact physically right after delivery. This is known as bonding. It appears to be important for the development of the babies, and it increases the attachment of the parents to the child. When parent-infant bonding takes place, there seems to be less chance of child abuse in later years.

In some hospital studies, there were mothers who avoided eye contact with their babies. They did not cuddle them and show interest in them the way most mothers did. Follow-up studies showed that these mothers were more apt to mistreat their children than those who related to their babies in the usual way. Mothers who seemed to have a high risk for abusing their babies were divided into two groups. One group was given special help in parenting, while the other was not. Abuse in the first group, although not eliminated, was less severe than in the second one.

It is not possible to make studies of all new mothers in and out of hospitals, nor does it seem wise to invade their privacy, but much can be done to encourage parent-infant bonding.

This is just one of many studies into the causes and prevention of child abuse. Finding the answers to ways of breaking the cycle can do much to prevent it.

Perhaps the teaching of parenting should begin with children in elementary school. Since children do not help with child care the way they did in earlier generations, many grow up and become parents with little or no idea of how to care for children. They are not exposed to wisdom that used to be passed down from one generation to the next. Even if grandmothers live in the same city as their children, the way they raised their babies may be entirely different from what is considered the right way today. For example, a grandmother may have given her baby a bottle every four hours, just as she was instructed to do by her doctor. The daughter who is breast-feeding her baby does so on demand.

Courses in parenting include more than what to

expect of an infant and child. Understanding feelings is important, too. Building self-esteem is an important part of parenting that does not change from one generation to the next. However, it is an art that seems to have been lost by many, and it is one that has been neglected. Most parents who abuse their children have low opinions of themselves, and their children grow up feeling the same way.

Self-esteem is not conceit. Conceit is a whitewash to cover low self-esteem. When you have high self-esteem, you feel good about yourself. You are glad you are you. Many experts feel that even battered children may become parents who are loving and caring if their environments are changed and they are helped to develop high self-esteem and competence.

You can help to prevent child abuse by improving your own self-esteem and that of people around you. If you have a friend who always downs himself or herself, help your friend to understand that one unpleasant or poor quality does not make a whole bad person.

Many children who are bossy, pushy, and overbearing are attempting to cover up their feelings of being worthless. People search for feelings of warmth, approval, closeness, and other good feelings in many ways. If parents do not supply them, children use various defenses in their search for them. Often, these defenses lead to further feelings of low self-esteem. Such persons make other people like them even less.

Karen's mother and father have the characteristics of many child abusers. They are too involved with their own needs to supply the support Karen needs, and Karen senses their rejection. She is the target of their abuse when their stress becomes too great. Karen finds that eating produces a good feeling, so she turns to food when her parents take their troubles out on her. She has eaten so much that she is very fat, and she hates herself. But the more she hates herself, the more she eats. Her parents make fun of her because she is so fat. So the cycle continues.

Since Karen is different from most children in her class, the others tease her. Perhaps if they accepted her for the many good qualities she has and encouraged her so that she felt better about herself, she would not have to stuff herself every time she felt upset. She would be less lonely, and she would not have to eat to make up for her lonely feelings.

Knowing that people can be mean because they are covering up feelings of low self-esteem can help you to get along with them. By yourself, you may not be able to break the cycle of child abuse in a case like Karen's, but everything you do to boost someone's self-esteem helps. If enough small actions are added together, they can make a big change.

Some people say that good parenting is just a question of doing what comes naturally. For those who have consciously or unconsciously learned good parenting skills, this may work very well. But to a father who has no idea of what to expect at his child's various ages, spanking, for example, may seem fitting for a six-month-old who is not toilet trained. Even though all children are different, many parents need to learn what to expect and not to expect from a child at various ages.

Learning how to teach young children is a part of parenting that is often neglected, and such ignorance may play a part in child abuse. For example, many mothers think that the best way to teach a baby not to bite is to bite the baby back. They think the baby will find out how much biting hurts and will stop. Actually, the baby is more apt to learn that Mother can hurt.

The use of violence as a form of teaching is widespread and is found in many school systems, but many experts believe that violence increases child abuse. This does not mean that a child who is spanked will necessarily become a child abuser, but spanking does teach violence as a way of life. Abusive and neglectful behavior is a complicated pattern of parenting. It is caused by many other things besides the childhood experiences of the parent.

Everyone can help to prevent child abuse by learning as much as possible about getting along with people and especially about being a parent. Perhaps you can convince a teacher or administrator in your school to teach a course on the subject of parenting.

The month of April has been designated as Child Abuse Prevention Month. This is a good time to work with organizations such as the Council for Children and Families or other groups in your community that are concerned about child abuse. You might sponsor a "No Hitters Day" in conjunction with your local baseball team, with pregame ceremonies urging the elimination of family violence. A month-long campaign might have the following objectives:

To help individuals acknowledge their own capacity for violence
To offer alternatives to dealing with rage
To acquaint people with community resources
To support action to reduce family violence

You might petition local television stations and theater groups to increase their time for family violence prevention programs and announcements during Child Abuse Prevention Month.

The designation of Child Abuse Prevention

Month is just one indication of increased awareness of the problem. Another indication of recognition of the importance of the prevention of child abuse is a report by the American Medical Association, published in the summer of 1985, urging physicians to go beyond the treatment of child abuse to try to *prevent* it from occurring. It is very rare for the AMA to put out guidelines like this on a single issue or disease. An important step in decreasing the amount of child abuse will be taken if doctors are prepared to identify situations in which abuse is likely and take steps to prevent it in these families.

Another indication of increased awareness and action toward prevention is the increase in education about sexual abuse. Media reporting about the hundreds of children in a small number of day-care centers across the United States who have suffered from sexual abuse has led to new concern. Millions of day-care centers have been operating with no licensing and with few questions asked by parents or other members of the community. With more than eleven million day-care centers in the United States, it is not surprising that there are not enough inspectors to monitor them all.

Today there is a movement toward better guidelines, including closer background checks on employees and volunteers, closer monitoring, and higher standards for day care in an effort to decrease the amount of abuse of children. Parents are assuming some responsibility for checking what goes on in the day-care centers to which they send their children.

The exposure of sexual abuse in some day-care centers has had some bad effects too. Now, there is fear that the sexual abuse scandals may discourage men from entering the field of early education. Some men worry that they will be typed as potential child molesters just because they want to work with children. Since most molesters do not have criminal records and appear to be fine citizens, screening of staff is a difficult problem.

Many parents and teachers are helping to prevent sexual abuse through education that goes far beyond the old approach of telling children to avoid strangers offering candy. Even young children are learning the difference between good touching and bad touching. They are told that the touching of private parts, those covered by bathing suits, should be reported to parents. And parents are increasingly willing to believe children who report such incidences. Children rarely lie about sexual abuse.

Teachers are using carefully prepared programs, including puppets, films, and coloring books, to alert children to potential abuse without frightening them. Such education, if done well, is no more frightening to children than education about preventing fire and avoiding traffic on busy streets.

Sexual abuse is a fact in society that has long been ignored, partly because many adults refused to admit that such ugly things could happen. The fact that the vast majority of abuse occurs in situations where the child knows and trusts the adult makes it even more difficult to face. A community and national consciousness is needed before good progress can be made in the problem of sexual abuse.

A special report by the Justice Department Task Force on Family Violence that was made public in the fall of 1984 gave many recommendations to help prevent child abuse. Some of them are:

> Congress should pass a law requiring background checks on volunteers and employees in all agencies that receive federal funding for the care and training of the young
>
> Police should make it a priority to arrest offenders of family violence rather than allow them to stay at home
>
> Cities should establish a system of safe-home networks in which citizens can provide temporary shelter to victims of abuse
>
> Local authorities should place tighter limits on an offender's access to victims, especially in sexual abuse and battering cases

> The government should give victims of family vio-
> lence priority for federally supported housing
> Courts should encourage procedures that make
> reporting less difficult for the victim

This last recommendation has already been put into action in some states. Many children who were abused suffered further abuse when they testified in court in the presence of the accused. For example, a six-year-old girl who testified that a preschool teacher had sexually molested her, then killed a turtle in her presence and told her that her parents would also be killed if she told what had happened, confessed that she was afraid to tell the truth in court. Her father pointed out that the presence of the abuser frightened the child.

In June 1985, the first legislation to allow simultaneous two-way closed television testimony for some children under the age of eleven was passed in California so that these children will not have to confront the person who abused them. A number of states now permit victims to give videotaped testimony either in trials or pretrial procedures to prevent further abuse of the victims. Using anatomically correct dolls to demonstrate molestation, admitting the hearsay testimony of parents, and other innovations are being introduced to prevent further abuse of children at the hands of the court.

Prevention of child abuse includes the prevention of kidnapping of children by noncustodial parents and by strangers. The problem of missing children has been called a national nightmare that strikes thousands of families each year. No one knows how many children are abused after they run away from their homes or are kidnapped, either by noncustodial parents or strangers. Many of the estimated children who are voluntarily missing, or labeled as runaways and throwaways, return home unharmed, but even these children are frequently victims of street crime and exploitation. Children who are stolen from one parent by the other often suffer physical abuse in addition to the emotional abuse that comes from such action. Estimates of this group of children vary from 25,000 to 500,000 per year. As many as 20,000 to 50,000 children are victims of kidnapping by strangers. Many missing children are never found, or are not found alive.

The pornography and prostitution of children are highly organized multimillion-dollar industries. Lee MacFarlane of the Children's Institute International in Los Angeles testified at a congressional hearing in 1984 that she believes there is a network of child molesters engaged in operating day-care centers. According to a report that was released in 1984 by the U.S. Justice Department, more than 1.5 million children under the age of sixteen were then involved in prostitution or child pornography. Certainly, major efforts are still needed to prevent the abuse of children by pornographers in spite of recent laws that attempt to do so.

The National Center for Missing and Exploited Children began its work in 1984. The center provides assistance to individuals, groups, agencies, and state and local governments in locating and returning missing children. It helps those concerned with preventing abuse of children by molesters, pornographers, prostitution rings, and other forms of criminal exploitation. And it promotes education and public awareness of child abuse.

Many people who want to help prevent child abuse have joined together in organizations such as the National Center for Missing and Exploited Children. You will find a list of these agencies at the back of the book. By contacting them, you can find many additional ways in which to help prevent child abuse.

8

Help for the Child
Who Cries Softly

The voices of thousands of abused children who cry softly are now being heard by teachers, doctors, nurses, neighbors, and friends at school. Would you know what to do if a friend told you about something that had happened to him or her that seemed to be an obvious case of abuse? Would you decide to stay away from that situation, since it was none of your business? Or would you report it?

Reporting can be scary. You may wonder if someone will blame you for telling tales. But if you are certain that a person is being abused, you should report it. Do not try to solve the problem yourself. Both the abused child and the parents need help from people who are trained to provide that kind of help.

If you think you should report a case of child abuse, be certain that you know the facts, then act. Many young people who know about a case of abuse find it helpful to share the problem with a parent, teacher, religious leader, or someone they feel will understand. If a person does not want to get involved, you might remind him or her that no one can be sued for reporting a case of child abuse if it is done in good faith. You have a responsibility to see that a report is made if you know someone is being abused.

If no one will help you, or if the person you ask for help does not know where to report child abuse, look in the blue pages of your telephone book, under Guide to Human Services, or in the white pages under Child Abuse. Perhaps your community has a child abuse hotline. If you cannot find any of these, call your local hospital and ask for Social Services, go to your local library, or try the local welfare department or public health authorities.

All fifty states have reporting laws. In some states it is against the law for certain people, such as doctors, dentists, teachers, and police, to ignore child abuse. Suppose a mother calls her doctor in the middle of the night because her daughter has come crying to her with an account of the father's fondling her in a way that made her feel uncomfortable. His physical affection for his child spilled over in the form of sexual contact. The mother is shocked, but she knows that her husband is sexually attracted to young children. Unlike many wives, she wants to protect her daughter, even if it means creating a problem between herself and her husband. The doctor asks to see the father at once, and he talks with him about the problem. He also mentions that he must report this case of child abuse and that the report will bring a visit from a social worker. He explains that his action is necessary by law, but this does not mean that the child will be taken from her home. It does mean that a social worker will work with the father to help him overcome his problem.

Even if you do not wish to report a case of abuse, you may be interested in finding out what the reporting laws are in your state. To do this, write to the Attorney General's Office at your state capitol building. The State Department of Welfare or Public Health may be able to provide you with some information on reporting abuse in your state.

One way to help children who are being abused is to make people aware of the need for reporting and let them know how to go about making a report. In one community, an awareness program increased the amount of reporting tremendously. But increased reporting can be a problem if there are not enough services to help the children and their parents.

What happens when a case of child abuse is reported? This depends on a number of things, but especially on the kind of help that is available in the community.

Take Jane, for example. A neighbor reported that a child was being abused and a social worker came to the house to check on the truth of the report. Jane was frightened when the stranger came, even though the social worker tried to make friends with her. Jane's mother started to cry. She told the worker that the cut on Jane's face came from an accident when Jane fell with a knife in her hand. Jane knew this was not so, but if she told the strange lady the truth, her father would certainly hurt her more. Besides, she loved her father and she did not want to get him in trouble.

Suppose the police would take her father to jail if they knew the truth! Suppose they would take Jane away from her parents! This would upset Jane far more than the cut on her face that her father had made with his penknife.

The social worker told Jane that she had come to help. She promised that she would try to teach Jane's father better ways of dealing with his anger. He would not be punished if he cooperated. The social worker said that she wanted to make life better for the whole family. Jane knew that her father often became angry, and he had lashed out at her many times. She did not want to hurt her father, but she had been thinking about running away. Jane, who had never learned how to trust, did not really trust this new person. But then, she was afraid to stay home and she was afraid to run away. So she took a chance and trusted this stranger.

The social worker suggested that Jane's father join a self-help group known as Parents Anonymous. Jane had heard about this group from announcements on the radio. She had asked her father to join several months before, but he would not talk to her about it. Now there were booklets that explained what happened at the meetings. Now he had to go or face going to court for child abuse.

Parents Anonymous is a self-help group for abusive parents that was begun in 1970 by a woman known as Jolly K., a child abuser, and Leonard Lieber, a mental health worker who was trying to help her. This organization has grown to include thousands of members in more than eight hundred chapters throughout the United States and in several other countries. The program features group meetings with a professional who volunteers to serve as a group adviser. Services are available to members twenty-four hours a day as a means of preventing child abuse. If you cannot locate a chapter in your community, or if you know people who would like to start a new chapter, write to the national headquarters of Parents Anonymous at 22330 Hawthorne Boulevard, Suite 208, Torrance.

California 90505. Or, if you know a parent who needs help and you cannot reach anyone, tell him or her to call one of these toll-free numbers: outside California, 1-800-421-0353; in California, 1-800-353-0368.

Jane's father attends a meeting of Parents Anonymous every Tuesday evening at the local Y. Many of the people who go to the meetings do not give their names, but they all talk freely about their problems. Here Jane's father is learning how to redirect his anger. Instead of hitting Jane, he pounds on chairs, hits the wall, and yells at the window when he explodes inside. He is trying not to discipline Jane when he is angry. He has learned to wait several hours, until he is calm enough to discipline her without losing control.

One of Jane's father's problems was not being able to reach out for help. After several meetings of Parents Anonymous, he became more comfortable and exchanged phone numbers with other members. Now he can contact others in the group, when he is upset, to talk with them about his feelings and to cool his anger. Sometimes he calls after he has handled a problem especially well, and each success makes the next one easier.

Jane's father is learning to look at himself differently and to repair the emotional damage that has been a burden to him for many years. Through Parents Anonymous, he and thousands of other people are improving their self-image, and this in turn improves their relationship with their children.

Parents find their way to Parents Anonymous through many routes. Some, such as Jane's father, are sent by doctors, social workers, or others because they have been reported as child abusers. Many parents join voluntarily after hearing about the group on television or radio. Some are referred by public and private agencies, such as the courts, police, and child protection agencies. Others hear of it through neighbors, friends, or relatives. In many cases, the group adviser or sponsor helps members to reach additional services, such as welfare assistance, family counseling, that they did not know about or were afraid to reach out for.

Parents Anonymous is praised highly by experts in the field of child abuse as well as by its members. It is a way of sharing angry feelings with others and of receiving suggestions about how to act. This costs nothing and does not risk exposure. It has helped to break the cycle of abuse in thousands of families.

Hotlines are another source of help for the child who cries quietly. Besides being a way of reporting for people who become aware of abuse, they serve many parents who report their own problems. A parent can get help from a hotline without having

to give a name, but many parents do identify themselves to an understanding listener.

The hotline listener is trained to listen to an
abusive parent without being critical. For example,
a mother feels she is losing control. She knows that
if her daughter makes one more mess, she will
throw the little girl across the room. She calls the
hotline number, and the person who answers says
she knows how upsetting children can be. The hotline worker listens to the mother without cutting
her off or shutting her out. She really hears how the
mother feels and knows what she is thinking. As
the mother talks out her anger and frustration, she
feels calmer. A few minutes later, when the child
upsets her cup of milk, her mother calmly gives her
a sponge and suggests that her daughter wipe it up.
Then she pours another glass of milk and feels
good about herself because she kept the situation
under control.

Hotline workers play a large part in referring
callers to community groups such as Parents
Anonymous where they can find long-term help. It
takes a long time to develop a better sense of self,
and this is one of the goals for preventing child
abuse.

Helplines are modeled after hotlines, but they
are especially concerned with children. Many helplines are part of programs at hospitals. Most of
them have volunteers who can visit a home where

there is a life-threatening situation. Others will contact a rescue squad, police, or similar protective services.

In some communities, family outreach centers work with people who may have a high potential for child abuse and neglect. One of their functions is to act as a support in times of tension and stress.

Crisis-care centers are safe shelters for children who have been abused or are in immediate danger because of a family crisis. Children are usually placed in such a center for two to four days. During this time, social workers and others can arrange a long-term plan of help for parents, and they can work to relieve the immediate tension. Crisis nurseries are open twenty-four hours a day so that a parent can leave a child there when the family is going through stress.

Crises and stress are common in the lives of all parents. Housing problems, unemployment, family arguments, separation from loved ones, and many other things can cause crises. Many child abusers lack self-confidence, imagination, and the knowledge of how to get help. A sudden crisis may be enough to push an already overwhelmed parent into abusing a child. Helping to relieve stress in the lives of parents is an important way in which young people can help to prevent child abuse.

When does discipline become child abuse? Dr. Catherine Chilman, professor at the School of Social Welfare, University of Wisconsin at Milwaukee, suggests that parents who are upset find it much harder to be loving but firm with children. She urges that parents get enough rest, enjoyment, and companionship for themselves. Unfortunately, many parents who abuse their children have never learned how to enjoy themselves.

Studies show that mothers who must be with their children constantly are more likely to react negatively toward them than mothers who have regular relief from their responsibilities as parents. Mothers are more likely to "blow hot and cold" with their children when they are confined with them over long periods of time.

How can you help prevent child abuse by relieving stress? Check with the family agencies in your community to see if there is a crisis nursery or day-care center where you can work as a volunteer. Even if a day-care center is for all children, you may help to prevent mistreatment by providing some relief for a mother who might become an abuser.

Young volunteers in day-care centers may help to prevent abuse for reasons other than the relief to overburdened parents. Dr. Jill Korban, a consultant on child abuse and neglect, feels there would be advantages in building day-care centers and elementary schools side by side. If school children were involved in the care of younger children, it could help develop their own self-esteem. It would also give them practice for their future roles as adults and parents. It would help to educate them about normal child development with its many individual differences. And it would provide parents with a source of help in their jobs as caretakers, relieving them from their constant responsibility.

Some organizations provide opportunities for young people to help on an individual basis. Big Brothers/Big Sisters of America is a national organization that is acutely aware of the problems faced by families under stress. Volunteers work with children and young people who are in need of friendship and guidance, and these volunteers have the support of trained social workers. If you are interested in helping in this way, or if you feel that a Big Brother or Big Sister could help you, call the local agency listed in your telephone directory or your local social service agency.

Julie belongs to a group that works to prevent child abuse by forming relationships with individuals. She visits Marie, a five-year-old girl whose mother used shaking as a form of discipline. Whenever it became too hard for Marie's mother to deal calmly with a situation, she shook baby Marie very hard. Marie's mother did not know that the brain inside a baby's head is not securely anchored. Now,

Marie has a vision problem because of the severe shaking.

Marie's mother never meant to hurt her baby. She was proud of the fact that she never hit her. She was only one of thousands of parents who do not realize that shaking is dangerous for young children and may result in brain damage or impaired vision. Now, Marie's mother is getting help from a social worker, and she has some time to herself so that she can unwind. When Julie comes, she takes Marie for walks, plays with her in the neighborhood park, and enjoys many happy hours with the little girl every week. Julie looks forward to the eager greetings and the love that Marie gives her.

No matter how you choose to help prevent child abuse, you can be certain that your help is badly needed. Community programs vary from none to very good, but even in cities with the finest programs in the world, only a limited number of abused children and their families can be helped by them.

An outstanding program that helps children in as many as twenty-six states is CASA (Court Appointed Special Advocate). The fate of abused and neglected children who must be placed outside the home may be a series of foster homes. Foster care, designed to be temporary, often becomes a permanent arrangement and frequently not a very good one. In 1976, when there were more than half a million children in the United States in foster care, Judge David W. Soukup, then Presiding Judge of King County Superior Court in Seattle, Washington, began to look for ways to make sure the cases of abused and neglected children were presented to the court in such a way that the child's best interests would be served. Traditionally, an attorney known as a "guardian ad litem" is appointed by the court to represent the child. Few such attorneys have the time or training needed for the comprehensive investigation that provides the information the court needs to make a wise decision.

Judge Soukup decided to recruit and train community volunteers who were willing to make a long-term commitment to every child for whom they would serve as guardians. CASA provided 110 trained people for 498 children in 1977, its first year. The Seattle program soon became a model for other programs as far away as Rhode Island, California, Arizona, Arkansas, Florida, and Connecticut. Florida was the first state to pass legislation authorizing such a program, but many other states have followed.

By 1985, there were more than one hundred CASA (or volunteer guardian ad litem) programs. Many states now have laws mandating the appointment of a volunteer CASA for abused and neglected children.

Consider a case like Karen's. She lived with her mother until her teacher became concerned about the burns that Karen tried to explain away with a variety of excuses. When the case was reported to the social service department in her community, the true cause of the burns became clear. Karen's mother really believed that she could teach Karen by burning her with a lighted cigarette when the little girl failed to remember to take out the trash or do the other chores that were assigned to her. The chores were numerous, and Karen could not possibly keep up with the work her mother thought she should do.

It seemed obvious that Karen needed to be placed in another home. Mrs. King, a CASA, was assigned at the first custody hearing. This volunteer investigated, evaluated, and recommended to the court what she believed to be truly in Karen's best interests, both from a temporary and a long-term standpoint.

Mrs. King spent much time interviewing Karen and her mother, she reviewed records, documents, and clinical data, and she presented the relevant facts to the court at hearings, through written reports and direct testimony. She was a negotiator, making sure that court, social services, and legal counsel all fulfilled their obligations to Karen. She monitored the court orders, ensuring compliance by all parties and bringing to the court's attention any changes in circumstances that required modification.

Mrs. King made a long-term commitment to be the eyes and ears of the court. She had trained along with other volunteers for many hours, learning about child abuse and its causes, juvenile justice legal procedures, foster care and placement, and the CASA role. Preservice training for CASA lasts from ten to forty-five hours and training continues while the volunteers begin their work with a case.

CASA Judy Sanders expressed the feeling of many when she said, "It's knowing that your efforts affected a child's life when he or she needed it most." CASA programs have been very successful in increasing the number of children returned to their families or placed in permanent homes, and in reducing their stay in foster care.

James Wooten, Deputy Administrator of the Office of Juvenile Justice and Delinquency Prevention, has said, "The CASA program provides the best opportunity I know for the citizen volunteer to radically improve an abused or neglected child's chance for happiness."

In some communities, mothers who abuse their children live at a shelter with their babies while a team of well-trained experts bring together many skills to help break the cycle of violence. Women learn how to be good mothers through actual demonstrations, while, at the same time, they themselves experience some of the mothering they missed as children. They may live at the shelter for months, and after they leave, the shelter staff keeps in close touch with them as they begin to live their lives again in the community. This type of program was pioneered at the New York Foundling Hospital under the direction of Dr. Vincent J. Fontana, who is well known for his work in the prevention and treatment of child abuse.

Day-care centers in many communities are helping both abusive mothers and their maltreated children. For example, at the Elizabeth Lund Home in Burlington, Vermont, children who have been abused are accepted for day care at the center on condition that a parent spend a full day every week there with them. As parents help with many of the children at the center under the direction of the staff, they learn to change their own violent and neglectful behavior. They also learn child-management skills and receive counseling on different ways to deal with stress.

Village of Childhelp is a residential care community for severely assaulted children that acts as a model for other programs. The Village consists of ten buildings on 120 acres of rural land in California that house children between the ages of two and twelve. These children have histories of various types of assault that place them at high risk of subsequently becoming juvenile delinquents and adult criminals if they do not get the kind of caring they need. Although not everyone agrees with the approach used at this residential community, its innovative and comprehensive interdisciplinary residential treatment program appears to have helped many of the more than two hundred assaulted children who have lived there. The Village itself is considered a laboratory for learning about effective intervention and prevention practices in the field of child abuse. National public education and other programs are part of Childhelp, an organization that is supported primarily by the private contributions of individuals, corporations, and foundations.

Recent research shows the importance of helping abused children at a very early age. Child abuse appears to influence behavior patterns in very young children according to a study by researchers Mary Mann and Carol George and a team of observers at the University of California at Berkeley. The actions of abused and nonabused children ages one to three years were observed and compared. It was found that abused children often responded to the distress of other children by abusing them further. Most nonabused children were sensitive to the pains of those around them and tried to comfort them. We have seen that many parents who abuse their children were abused themselves when they were young. Early treatment can help to break this cycle of abuse.

The first effects of parental neglect are frequently noticeable shortly after birth. One approach to helping neglected children is working with the children rather than the parents. Many neglectful parents are resistant to change. They are distrustful of outsiders, often have alcohol or other drug problems, and may need nurturing themselves. Change in the kind of care provided by parents, if it does come, comes slowly. Many social workers find that they can accomplish more in the limited time they have available by working directly with the children as soon as they are identified. Many children can overcome the effects of neglect when they have caring adults other than their parents to guide them.

Some of the mistreated children who live in the area of Denver, Colorado, are part of an outstanding program. These activities at the National Center for the Prevention and Treatment of Child Abuse and Neglect draw visitors from all over the world. Among the projects are live-in programs, a twenty-four-hour crisis nursery, a play school for abused children that is in session six hours a day, and a program with people who have been successful parents and who are willing to make home visits to parents who need support.

Education and training for doctors, nurses, social workers, and others who can help is a part of the Denver program. There are thousands of social welfare departments throughout the United States, and many of them are finding help through the National Center's publications.

Sometimes the support of nonprofessionals plays a very important part in helping abused children and adolescents. Dr. Robert Friedman of the Florida Mental Health Institute suggests that informal personal relationships may be vital to an abused adolescent. Having support from a friend, teacher, coach, counselor, or friend's parent with whom the young person can feel accepted and can "practice being likable" can help an abused teenager become an emotionally healthy adult. You may be that friend who makes an important difference in the life of someone who has been abused or neglected.

Just some of the ways of helping abused children and adolescents have been mentioned in this chapter. You may be able to help by encouraging teacher, student, and community involvement. Organizing peer counseling programs, poster-making, or being an advocate for children in any way makes a contribution to the cause.

There is an urgent need for more people to listen

for the child who cries softly. There is an urgent need for more people to become involved with the problem of child abuse in general. You can help make people aware that child abuse hurts everyone.

Hotlines

Childhelp
1-800-4-A-CHILD
For help in reporting child abuse.

National Center for Missing and Exploited Children
1-800-843-5678
To report a missing child or give information that could help in a child's recovery.

National Runaway Switchboard
1-800-621-4000
Help for runaway children.

Parents Anonymous
1-800-421-0353 (except in California)
1-800-353-0368 in California
For information or for the location of a chapter in your community

Suggestions for Further Reading

Fiction

Adler, Carole S. *Down by the River.* G. P. Putnam's Sons, 1981. Ages 12 and up.

Anderson, Mary. *Step on a Crack.* Atheneum Publishers, 1979. Ages 12 to 15.

Armstrong, Louise. *Saving the Big-Deal Baby.* E. P. Dutton & Co., 1980. Ages 10 and up.

Ashley, Bernard. *A Break in the Sun.* S. G. Phillips, 1980. Ages 11 and up.

Bauer, Marion. *Foster Child.* Dell Publishing Co., 1977. Ages 11 and up.

Bradbury, Bianca. *Those Traver Kids.* Houghton Mifflin Co., 1972. Ages 9 to 12.

Bulla, Clyde Robert. *Almost a Hero.* E. P. Dutton & Co., 1981. Ages 11 and up.

Culin, Charlotte. *Cages of Glass, Flowers of Time.* Bradbury Press, 1979. Ages 12 and up.

Dodson, Susan. *Have You Seen This Girl?* Four Winds Press, 1982. Ages 13 and up.

Greene, Bette, *The Summer of My German Soldier.* Bantam Books, 1974. Grades 7 and up.

Greene, Sheppard M. *The Boy Who Drank Too Much.* Dell Publishing Co., 1980. Ages 12 and up.

Hill, Margaret. *Turn the Page, Wendy.* Abingdon Press, 1981. Ages 10 to 14.

Hunt, Irene. *The Lottery Rose.* Grosset & Dunlap, 1978. Grades 12 and up.

Moeri, Louise. *The Girl Who Lived on the Ferris Wheel.* Avon Books, 1980. Ages 13 and up.

Rabe, Bernice. *Rass.* Thomas Nelson, 1973. Ages 10 to 14.

Roberts, Willo D. *Don't Hurt Laurie!* Atheneum Publishers, 1977. Ages 10 to 13.

Smith, Doris B. *Tough Chauncey.* William Morrow & Co., 1974. Ages 11 to 15.

Strang, Celia. *Foster Mary.* McGraw-Hill Book Co., 1979. Ages 10 to 13.

Whelan, Gloria. *A Time to Keep Silent.* G. P. Putnam's Sons, 1979. Ages 11 to 14.

Nonfiction

For Younger Readers

Cohen, Daniel, and Susan Cohen. *Teenage Stress: Understanding the Tensions You Feel.* ... M. Evans & Co., 1984.

Hyde, Margaret O. *Foster Care and Adoption.* Franklin Watts, 1982.

————. *Is This Kid "Crazy"? Understanding Unusual Behavior.* Westminster Press, 1983.

————. *Sexual Abuse—Let's Talk About It.* Westminster Press, 1984.

Hyde, Margaret O., and Lawrence E. Hyde. *Missing Children.* Franklin Watts, 1985.

Wheat, Patte. *You're Not Alone: Kid's Book on Alcoholism and Child Abuse.* National Committee for Prevention of Child Abuse, 1985.

For Older Readers

Abrahms, Sally. *Children in the Crossfire: The Tragedy of Parental Kidnapping.* Atheneum Publishers, 1983.

Dolan, Edward F., Jr. *Child Abuse.* Franklin Watts, 1980.

Finkelhor, David. *Child Sexual Abuse: New Theory and Research.* Free Press, 1984.

Fisher, Nancy. *Reaching Out: The Volunteer in Child Abuse and Neglect Programs.* National Center on Child Abuse and Neglect, U.S. Department of Health, Education, and Welfare, 1979.

Garbarino, James, and Anne C. Garbarino. *Maltreatment of Adolescents.* National Committee for Prevention of Child Abuse, 1982.

Halperin, Michael. *Helping Maltreated Children: School and Community Involvement.* C. V. Mosby Co., 1979.

Meier, John H., ed. *Assault Against Children: Why It Happens and How to Stop It.* College-Hill Press, 1985.

Straus, Murray A., Richard J. Gelles, and Suzanne K. Steinmetz. *Behind Closed Doors: Violence in the American Family.* Doubleday & Co., Anchor Books, 1981.

Williams, Gertrude J., and John Money, eds. *Traumatic Abuse and Neglect of Children at Home.* Johns Hopkins University Press, 1980.

Pamphlets

For current catalogs of inexpensive publications write to:

National Center on Child Abuse and Neglect
Children's Bureau
Administration for Children, Youth, and Families
U.S. Department of Health and Human Services
P.O. Box 1182
Washington, DC 20013

National Committee for Prevention of Child Abuse
332 South Michigan Avenue, Suite 1250
Chicago, IL 60604

National Organizations Concerned with Child Abuse

Al-Anon Family Group Headquarters
One Park Avenue
New York, NY 10016
See the white pages in your telephone book for local groups.

American Humane Association
Child Protection Division
9725 East Hampden Street
Denver, CO 80231

Big Brothers-Big Sisters of America
230 North 13th Street
Philadelphia, PA 19107

Boys Town, U.S.A.
Communications and Public Service Division
Boys Town, NE 68010

Center of Child Advocacy and Protection
1341 G Street NW
Washington, DC 20005

Child Abuse Listening Mediation, Inc. (CALM)
P.O. Box 718
Santa Barbara, CA 93102

Childhelp USA/International
6463 Independence Avenue
Woodland Hills, CA 91370

Child Welfare League of America
67 Irving Place
New York, NY 10003

Children's Institute International
701 South New Hampshire Avenue
Los Angeles, CA 90005

National Center for Missing and Exploited Children
1835 K Street NW, Suite 700
Washington, D.C. 20006

National Center on Child Abuse and Neglect (NCCAN)
Children's Bureau
Administration for Children, Youth, and Families
U.S. Department of Health and Human Services
P.O. Box 1182
Washington, DC 20013

National Committee for Prevention of Child Abuse
332 South Michigan Avenue, Suite 1250
Chicago, IL 60604

National Council of Jewish Women
15 East 26th Street
New York, NY 10010

National Council of Juvenile
and Family Court Judges
University of Nevada
Box 8978
Reno, NV 89507

Parents Anonymous (PA)
22330 Hawthorne Boulevard, Suite 208
Torrance, CA 90505

SCAN (Suspected Child Abuse and Neglect)
Volunteer Services
2500 North Tyler Street
Little Rock, AR 72217

Index

About the Author

Margaret O. Hyde is the author of an outstanding list of books for young people. Published by The Westminster Press are *Sexual Abuse: Let's Talk About It; Is This Kid "Crazy"? Understanding Unusual Behavior;* and *Cancer in the Young: A Sense of Hope,* with Lawrence E. Hyde. Mrs. Hyde has written documentaries for NBC-TV and taught children, young adults, and adults.

In preparing *Cry Softly! The Story of Child Abuse,* Margaret Hyde had the help of a wide variety of people, including abused children, their parents, doctors who work with these people, and persons in organizations that research this subject.